PENGUIN BOOKS

# Test Your Phrasal Verbs

# Test
# Your
# Phrasal
# Verbs

**Jake Allsop**

**Illustrated by Ross Thomson
and Terry Burton**

PENGUIN ENGLISH

PENGUIN BOOKS
Published by the Penguin Group
Penguin Books Ltd, 27 Wrights Lane, London W8 5TZ, England
Penguin Books USA Inc., 375 Hudson Street, New York, New York 10014, USA
Penguin Books Australia Ltd, Ringwood, Victoria, Australia
Penguin Books Canada Ltd, 10 Alcorn Avenue, Toronto, Ontario, Canada M4V 3B2
Penguin Books (NZ) Ltd, 182–190 Wairau Road, Auckland 10, New Zealand

Penguin Books Ltd, Registered Offices: Harmondsworth, Middlesex, England

First published 1990
10 9 8 7 6 5 4 3

Filmset in Century Schoolbook

Printed and bound in Great Britain by
BPCC Hazell Books
Aylesbury, Bucks, England
Member of BPCC Ltd

# CONTENTS

# INTRODUCTION

The book is divided into five sections, each containing tests of a similar type, as follows.

The first test in each section [1,11,21,31,41] tests a range of phrasal verbs using the common verbs *come, take, get, go* and *be*. The second [2,12,22,32,42] puts a variety of interesting phrasal verbs into situations and asks you to work out from the context what they mean. The third [3,13,23,33,43] tests a range of phrasal verbs using the common particles *away, down, in, off* and *out*. The fourth [4,14,24,34,44] tests phrasal verbs which have the pattern *verb + adverb + preposition*. The fifth [5,15,25,35,45] provides situations and asks you to supply or define the phrasal verbs in them. The sixth [6,16,26,36,46] deals with fifty phrasal verbs which have more than one meaning and tests them in contexts such as matching pairs of sentences and cartoons. The seventh [7,17,27,37,47] is quite searching, for it asks you to complete sentences by selecting, from a choice of four phrasals, the one which **best** fits the situation. In some cases, other alternatives would fit, but are not as good. The eighth [8,18,28,38,48] is designed to provide a bit of amuse-ment – and puzzlement – by asking you to find one-letter spelling mistakes in newspaper headlines. The ninth [9,19,29,39,49] deals with nouns and adjectivals formed from phrasal verbs, a very important feature of English. The tenth [10,20,30,40,50] provides some more light relief by offering you some crosswords and similar word games involving phrasal verbs.

The tests are designed to produce lively and interactive group work when used in class but have been constructed to allow the keen student to work on his/her own (keys to all the tests are available at the end of the book).

In writing this book, I freely acknowledge my debt to Peter Watcyn-Jones, who first created the *Test Yourself* series and set a high standard. If this book in the *Test Yourself* series is only half as witty and wise as his, I shall be well pleased.

Jake Allsop   Cambridge   Spring 1989

## TO THE STUDENT

This book will help you to learn a lot of new English words. But in order for the new words to become "fixed" in your mind, you need to test yourself again and again. Here is one method you can use to help you learn the words:
1. Read through the instructions carefully for the test you are going to try. Then try the test, writing your answers **in pencil**.
2. When you have finished, check your answers and correct any mistakes you have made. Read through the test again, paying special attention to the words you didn't know or got wrong.
3. Try the test again five minutes later. You can do this either by covering up the words (for example, in the picture tests) or by asking a friend to test you. Repeat this until you can remember all the words.
4. **Rub out your answers**.
5. Try the test again the following day. (You should remember most of the words.)
6. Finally, plan to try the test at least twice again within the following month. After this most of the words will be "fixed" in your mind.

# 1 Phrasal verbs with COME

*Complete these sentences by adding the correct particle from the list below. Use each word once only.*

| | | | | |
|---|---|---|---|---|
| about | back | from | off | round |
| across | before | in | on | to |
| along | forward | into | out | up |

1   F comes ................... G in the alphabet.

2   Please come ...................! Make yourself at home.

3   A boomerang is a hunting weapon. It is supposed to come ................... to the person who throws it.

4   Just look at these old photographs. I came ................... them when I was clearing out an old cupboard.

5   Why don't you come ................... to our house for dinner on Saturday?

6   "What magazine is that?"
    "It's a literary magazine called the *Bookworm*."
    "How often does it come ...................?"
    "Monthly."

7   The sergeant asked for volunteers, but only three came ................... .

8   "Where do you come ...................?"
    "Thailand."

9   Pollution, war, the greenhouse effect, the ozone layer: I don't know what the world is coming ................... .

10   "Come ..................., Philip. Everyone else has finished except you!"

11   We're all going out for a pizza. Would you like to come ...................?

12   I hear that John has come ................... a lot of money. Apparently, a rich aunt of his has died and left him half a million pounds.

13   Every time the subject of holidays comes ..................., Ruth and her husband have an argument.

14   Paul is working on a plan to convert his farmhouse into a bed-and-breakfast place. He reckons he'll make a fortune if it comes ................... .

15   There has been another big crash on the M25 motorway. How did it come ...................?

# 2 Definitions

*Choose the alternative which best matches the meaning of the underlined phrasal verb.*

1   I need twenty pounds to <u>tide me over</u> until the end of the month.

   **a**   cover my expenses   **b**   pay off my debts   **c**   spend   **d**   borrow

2   It was getting late so I decided to <u>turn in.</u>

   **a**   give up   **b**   go to bed   **c**   switch off the light   **d**   go home

3   They had a quarrel one evening, but they <u>patched things up</u> next morning.

   **a**   hid their feelings from each other   **b**   repaired the broken furniture
   **c**   made things worse by continuing the quarrel
   **d**   settled their differences

4   She had such a bad cold that I was not surprised she <u>dozed off</u> in the middle of the afternoon.

   **a**   forgot to take her medicine   **b**   fell asleep   **c**   felt very ill
   **d**   went home early

5   Don't buy the first thing you see: <u>shop around</u> a bit.

   **a**   go to several different shops to compare prices
   **b**   try to find the cheapest one
   **c**   look at everything they have got in the shop
   **d**   wait until you know exactly what you want

6   Anne wanted to go to the ball, and poor old Andy had to <u>cough up</u> fifty pounds for the tickets.

   **a**   reluctantly pay   **b**   easily save up   **c**   confidently ask for
   **d**   unwillingly borrow

7   Bill had to <u>dip into</u> his savings account to pay for his holiday.

   **a**   increase   **b**   close   **c**   take money from   **d**   put money into

8   The whole group were going on a picnic, and they said that I could <u>tag along</u> if I wanted.

   **a**   pay for the drinks   **b**   walk behind them   **c**   go with them
   **d**   carry the picnic basket

9   My father <u>ticked me off</u> because I used his electric razor.

   **a**   reprimanded me   **b**   was proud of me   **c**   laughed at me
   **d**   congratulated me

10   My speech started well, but I <u>dried up</u> after a few minutes.

   **a**   forgot what I wanted to say   **b**   couldn't continue
   **c**   decided to cut it short   **d**   began to feel thirsty

# 3 Phrasal verbs with AWAY

*Complete these sentences by adding the correct verb from the list below. (In some cases, you will need to change the tense or form of the verb.) Use each verb once only.*

| break | give | pass | slip | throw |
|-------|------|------|------|-------|
| drive | keep | run | stay | tow |
| fade | look | send | take | tuck |

1 Several children had to ................... away from school because of the bus strike.

2 We decided to ................... away from the main party and form a new party of our own called the Lunatic Party.

3 I didn't want to disturb anyone, so I just ................... away quietly without saying goodbye.

4 Did you ever play that silly game of knocking on someone's door and then ................... away?

5 If you park illegally in London, the police will either clamp your car or ................... it away.

6 "Old soldiers never die; they simply ................... away" (song).

7 They say that the Old Manor House is haunted by ghosts, but I think that it is only a story designed to ................... children away.

8 "I'd like a pizza marinara, please."
"To eat here or to ................... away?"

9 "Where are my jeans?"
"They were torn so I ................... them away."

10 A few years ago, everyone wanted a Rubik's Cube. Now you couldn't ................... them away.

11 The car that hit a child on a level crossing ................... away without stopping.

12 If you don't like having injections, it is a good idea to ................... away when the doctor sticks the needle into your arm.

13 She may look as if she hadn't got two pennies to rub together, but I bet she's got quite a bit of money ................... away somewhere.

14 An old tramp knocked on the door of the farmhouse and asked for something to eat, but the farmer's wife ................... him away empty-handed.

15 "Grandfather ................... away recently. He was ninety-three years old."
"What did he die of?"
"He was shot by a jealous husband."

# 4 Three-part phrasal verbs

*Match each phrasal verb in column A with a word or phrase in column B to give a common phrase. Then find a verb in column C which defines each phrasal verb.*

**Column A**
1 come in for
2 go in for
3 sit in on
4 stand in for
5 fall in with
6 give in to
7 tune in to
8 listen in on
9 cash in on
10 drop in on

**Column B**
a another's lesson
b temptation
c an opportunity
d a lot of criticism
e friends
f a sport or hobby
g other people's conversation
h somebody else's plans
i an absent colleague
j a programme on the radio

**Column C**
i find
ii substitute for
iii observe
iv exploit
v yield to
vi visit
vii receive
viii show support for
ix pursue
x eavesdrop

# 5  Definitions

*Use these verbs and particles to make up phrasal verbs which replace the definitions underlined in the sentences.*

VERBS: break  carry  clear
draw  fill  give  make
put  step  turn

PARTICLES: away  down
forward  in  off  out
up  up  up  up

1  I hate people who <u>reveal</u> the end of a film that you haven't seen.

2  With the introduction of computerised systems, we have been able to <u>increase</u> production by 25 per cent.

3  An ordinary soldier is expected to <u>obey</u> a superior officer's orders without question.

4  Harry says he intends to <u>end</u> his engagement to Naomi because she always opens her boiled eggs at the wrong end.

5  I'm glad that we have been able to <u>resolve</u> our little misunderstanding.

6  Before we do anything else, we ought to <u>prepare</u> a plan of action.

7  If you haven't got a genuine excuse for being late, you'll simply have to <u>invent</u> one.

8  Our society has become so bureaucratic that you even have to <u>complete</u> a form before you are allowed to die.

9  As nobody seems to know what to do next, may I <u>make</u> a proposal?

10  Ann is very upset: the Coal Board intends to <u>reject</u> her application to become a miner on the grounds that she is too tall.

# 6 Phrasal verbs with two meanings

*Each sentence in the first group uses the same phrasal verb as a sentence in the second group. Find the pairs of sentences by putting the following verbs into the sentences.*

| catch on   dry up   fall off   fall through   look up   make up   put off |
| run across   see through   take back |

1  There's a hole in the floor. Mind you don't ................ .................... it.

2  Whenever there is a period without rain, all the lakes ..................
...................... .

3  They said that the blue cheese was very tasty, but the smell .................. me
...................... .

4  They quarrel every morning, but they always kiss and ..................
...................... afterwards.

5  I've had some bad luck lately, but things are beginning to ..................
......................, I'm glad to say.

6  Once you have started something, you ought to .................. it .................. to
the end.

7  Hold the handlebars with both hands or you might .................. .................... .

8  This coat I bought is too small for me. Do you think I should .................. it
.................... to the shop?

9  Have you seen Roger lately? Yes, I happened to .................. .................... him
in Oxford last week.

10  Janet's children are very intelligent. When you explain something to them,
they seem to .................. .................... very quickly.

a  If you don't know the meaning of a word, you can always .................. it
.................. in the dictionary.

b  Is that a true story, or did you just .................. it ..................?

c  Sword swallowing is very popular in Albania, they tell me. Do you think it
would ever .................. .................... in this country?

d  Actors hate it when they forget their words and simply ..................
...................... .

e  It is dangerous to let children .................. .................... busy roads.

f  He tried to deceive her with his talk about marriage, but she was able to
.................. .................... him very easily.

g  We've made all the arrangements. Let's hope our plans don't ..................
.................. at the last moment.

**h** I said that Julie was a lazy good-for-nothing, but I was wrong: I .................
.................... everything I said about her.

**i** We used to get a lot of people at our meetings, but attendance has started to
.................... .................... lately.

**j** The meeting that was due to take place today has been ...................
.................... until next week.

# 7 Sentence completion

*Choose the phrasal verb which best completes the sentence.*

1   I was so tired that I just .................. .................. in the armchair.

   **a** flaked out   **b** broke up   **c** dropped out   **d** fell over

2   The subject of sex equality seems to .................. .................. in every discussion lesson in my school.

   **a** burst out   **b** zero in   **c** crop up   **d** harp on

3   I don't know whether Peter would be interested in joining our Conservation Society. I'll .................. him .................. about it.

   **a** chat up   **b** sound out   **c** tell off   **d** spur on

4   The new office block .................. .................. well with its surroundings.

   **a** blends in   **b** stands out   **c** shaped up   **d** sets off

5   "Isn't it terrible weather for spring?" .................. .................. summer!

   **a** Slope off   **b** Snap up   **c** Splash out   **d** Roll on

6   Our teacher tends to .................. .................. certain subjects which she finds difficult to talk about.

   **a** boil down   **b** string along   **c** skate over   **d** track down

7   It's a good idea to .................. .................. people before taking them into your confidence.

   **a** tumble to   **b** root out   **c** bank on   **d** size up

8   Some people can just .................. .................. a cold, but my colds seem to linger for weeks.

   **a** shrug off   **b** cough up   **c** pull through   **d** stamp out

9   The man in the market was selling leather coats very cheaply: they were such bargains that they were soon .................. .................. .

   **a** cleared off   **b** done for   **c** bought out   **d** snapped up

10  I couldn't remember where I had left my car, when it suddenly .................. .................. me that I didn't have a car any longer!

   **a** dawned on   **b** ran into   **c** went through   **d** tumbled to

# 8 Headlines

*The phrasal verbs in these headlines each contain a one-letter spelling mistake, for instance:* "MAN PRESSED UP AS WOMAN ARRESTED IN PARK", *which should be* "MAN DRESSED UP AS WOMAN ARRESTED IN PARK". *To help you find the mistakes, here is a checklist of the wrong and right letters (given in alphabetical order).*

The wrong letters: B C C G I L P R R U

The right letters:  D I L N N S T T W Y

1 PLUMBING COMPANY IN FINANCIAL DIFFICULTIES. "WE WILL HAVE TO LAG OFF MORE WORKERS UNLESS BUSINESS IMPROVES," SAYS BOSS

2 SCOTS TERRIER REFUSES TO LEAVE GRAVESIDE: HE IS "PIPING FOR HIS MASTER," SAYS VICAR

3 BIGAMOUS WOMAN BORN BETWEEN TWO HUSBANDS: "I JUST COULDN'T CHOOSE BETWEEN THEM," SHE TELLS JUDGE

4 CHANCELLOR HUNTS AT BIG TAX CUTS IN HIS NEXT BUDGET

5 OUTBREAK OF MYSTERY ILLNESS AIDS TO HOSPITAL'S PROBLEMS: "JUST NOT ENOUGH NURSES TO COPE WITH THE SITUATION"

6 ANGRY MOTHERS DEMAND MAXIMUM SENTENCE FOR CHILD KIDNAPPER: "HE OUGHT TO BE COCKED UP IN PRISON FOR THE REST OF HIS LIFE," THEY SAY

7 BRITISH ATHLETE INTENDS TO CRY FOR NEW WORLD RECORD AT COMING COMMONWEALTH GAMES

8 LEADING OFFICIAL RUMS UP TOWN PLAN IN ONE WORD: "DISGUSTING"

9 HOUSEWIVES TIRED OF BEING TIED TO THE KITCHEN SINK: THERE MUST BE MORE TO LIFE THAN LASHING UP, THEY SAY

10 EIGHTY-YEAR-OLD JUDGE CRITICISED FOR RODDING OFF DURING TRIAL. "IF HE CAN'T STAY AWAKE, HE SHOULD RETIRE," LAWYER COMMENTS

# 9 Nouns from phrasal verbs

*Nouns can be formed from phrasal verbs. Make the noun which completes the phrase under each picture, using these particles and verbs.*

VERBS: break break check hang hold lay tail take turn write

PARTICLES: away back by down off out out over through up

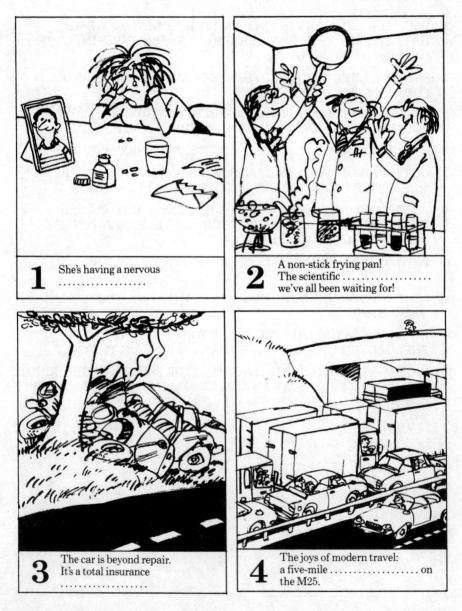

**1** She's having a nervous
...................

**2** A non-stick frying pan! The scientific ................... we've all been waiting for!

**3** The car is beyond repair. It's a total insurance
...................

**4** The joys of modern travel: a five-mile ................... on the M25.

**5** If the traffic gets too bad, pull into a .................. and have a rest.

**6** It takes minutes to fill your basket and hours to get through the supermarket ................

**7** If you don't feel like cooking go and get something from a Chinese ..................

**8** The Liverpool versus Machester United match always gets a record ..................

**9** A bank ..................

**10** If you drink too much, you will have a terrible .................. next morning.

# 10 Crossword puzzle

*Look at the clues and fill in the crossword below. We have put in a few letters to give you a start.*

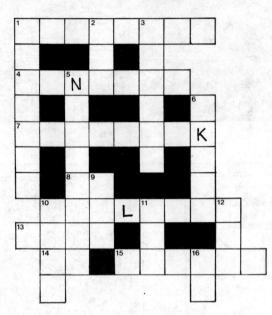

## ACROSS

1 Go up one side of the mountain and ..................... ..................... the other side (4,4)

4 If you want something from the mail-order catalogue, you will have to ..................... ..................... for it (4,3)

7 When a typhoid epidemic breaks out, we say there has been an ..................... of typhoid (8)

8 Verb used in the expression "..................... away with" (meaning "get rid of") (2)

10 A phrasal verb from the game of cricket. If somebody finds you very attractive, we say that you have .....................ed them ..................... (The verb describes the way the ball is sent to the batsman.) (4,4)

13 Opposite of "up" (4)

14 Opposite of "off" (2)

15 You use this to tie up parcels (6)

## DOWN

1 ...................-................... clothing is clothing which you no longer want (4, -3)

2 If you break the law, you may finally ................... up in jail (3)

3 A method of printing (6)

5 If you want to remember exactly what someone said, don't rely on your memory: ................... it ................... (4,4)

6 When you ................... on thin ice, you are in danger of going through and into deep water (5)

9 To "................... up" is to admit that you did something wrong. (3)

10 Restaurants in Wellington usually fill up very quickly on Saturday, so it is a good idea to phone up and ................... a table (4)

11 The opposite of 16dn. (It is also the first part of 7ac.) (3)

12 If you see the train about to leave the station, you will have to ................... to catch it. (The same verb is used in the expression "to ................... somebody down", meaning to criticise them or give them a bad name.) (3)

16 A particle used in many phrasal verbs, such as "turn ...................", meaning to go to bed, and "give ...................", meaning to surrender (2)

# 11 Phrasal verbs with TAKE

*Complete these sentences by adding the correct particle from the list below.*

| after | down | in | out | to |
|-------|------|-----|------|-----|
| back | for | off | over | up |
| back | in | on | to | up |

1   The Worldwide Chemicals Company was recently taken .................. by its biggest rival.

2   I'm not very fit, so I've decided to take .................. an active hobby such as squash or jogging.

3   I thought your wife and mine would not have much in common, but they seem to have taken .................. each other very well.

4   "Why have you taken .................. all the pictures in the sitting-room?"
    "Because I'm going to decorate it."

5   Is the *Bookworm* a very good magazine? Because, if it is, I might take .................. a subscription.

6   The new pizza restaurant is a great success. It's really taken .................. .

7   "Give me a kiss!"
    "What do you take me ..................? I'm a married girl!"

8   One day I painted little red spots all over my face, and told my father I had caught measles. For a moment he was completely taken .................., then he realised it was a joke.

9   "This radio I bought only picks up Radio Ulan Bator."
    "Why don't you take it .................. to the shop where you bought it, then?"

10  "Dad, is it all right if I leave school and get married?"
    "I can't advise you on that. You'd better take it .................. with your mother."

11  "Does John take .................. his mother or his father?"
    "Well, he looks just like his father, but he has his mother's nature."

12  Janet is secretary of four different clubs and chairman of two other societies. I think she has taken too much .................. .

13  This skirt is very loose. I think I'll have to take it .................. at the waist.

14  I'm sorry I said all those terrible things about you. I take them all .................. .

15  What's wrong with Kate? She used to be such a quiet girl, but she's taken .................. going out every night.

# 12 Definitions

*Choose the alternative which best matches the meaning of the underlined phrasal verb.*

1 As it was getting late, I decided to <u>press on.</u>

   **a** find a place to sleep    **b** phone for help    **c** finish the ironing
   **d** keep going

2 He had no business there, so I told him to <u>clear off.</u>

   **a** do the dishes    **b** leave at once
   **c** return everything to its proper place    **d** find something useful to do

3 I'm sorry to <u>butt in</u>, but I couldn't help overhearing what you said.

   **a** interrupt you    **b** contradict you    **c** speak so rudely to you
   **d** stop you

4 I didn't want to do it, but the other boys <u>egged</u> me <u>on.</u>

   **a** threw eggs at me    **b** called me names    **c** encouraged me
   **d** lifted me off the ground

5 The policeman <u>shot off</u> before anyone could stop him.

   **a** left in a hurry
   **b** let everyone know the truth about what was happening
   **c** fired his gun    **d** closed all the doors

6 Have you managed to <u>track down</u> that book I asked you about?

   **a** sell    **b** find    **c** read through    **d** get back

7 I know Sarah said she would lend you some money, but I wouldn't <u>bank on</u> it if I were you.

   **a** borrow from her    **b** spend the money all at once
   **c** save the money    **d** depend on her to do it

8 Whenever he makes a mistake, my boss always <u>trots out</u> the same old excuses.

   **a** shyly offers    **b** hotly denies    **c** carefully avoids
   **d** glibly produces

9 We <u>tarted up</u> the house in order to be able to sell it quickly.

   **a** offered at a low price    **b** advertised widely
   **c** decorated cheaply and quickly    **d** refurnished expensively

10 He looked really <u>washed out</u> after his operation.

   **a** very clean    **b** soaking wet    **c** very tired and pale
   **d** as if he had nowhere to live

# 13 Phrasal verbs with DOWN

*Complete these sentences by adding the correct verb from the list below. (In some cases, you will need to change the tense or form of the verb.) Use each verb once only.*

| | | | | |
|---|---|---|---|---|
| break | keep | put | shut | track |
| burn | let | settle | step | turn |
| cut | lie | shout | take | wear |

1   Some people think that the Queen should ................... down and allow Prince Charles to become King.

2   I asked Julia to marry me, but she ................... me down.

3   As soon as a leak of radioactive waste was discovered, the government ordered the plant to be ................... down.

4   "................... down or they'll see you!"

5   It has become much easier to ................... down trees in the Amazon rainforests since the introduction of the chainsaw.

6   She spent several months trying to find the famous artist Renos Demetrios. She finally ................... him down, though: he was living in a small hotel on the island of Shevtalia.

7   After several hours of questioning, the suspect finally ................... down and confessed to being the leader of the Malignant Dwarfs Party.

8   I found the novel *War and Peace* so exciting that, once I had picked it up, I simply couldn't ................... it down again until I had finished it.

9   "Anything you say will be ................... down and may be used in evidence against you" (police warning).

10  The steps were ................... down by the millions of feet that had trodden on them.

11  "Don't forget to be there at eight precisely."
    "Don't worry, you can depend on me: I won't ................... you down."

12  If you're not feeling well, go and ................... down for a while.

13  Isn't it time you stopped being an eternal teenager? Isn't it time you got your hair cut, got a job, got married and ................... down?

14  When he was asked why he had set fire to the bishop's palace, the Earl of Oxford replied: "I only ................... it down because I knew that the bishop was inside at the time."

15  At public meetings, there are two kinds of hecklers: those who want to ask difficult questions and to hear what the speaker has to say, and those who try to prevent him from speaking by ................... him down.

# 14 Three-part phrasal verbs

*Match each phrasal verb in column A with a word or phrase in column B to give a common phrase. Then find a verb in column C which defines each phrasal verb.*

**Column A**
1  come down with
2  cut down on
3  look down on
4  get down to
5  be down to
6  be up on
7  check up on
8  end up in
9  stand up for
10  come up against

**Column B**
a  people who are beneath you
b  your specialist subject
c  a difficulty
d  expenses
e  your beliefs
f  prison
g  your last penny
h  someone's movements
i  influenza
j  hard work

**Column C**
i  investigate
ii  apply yourself to
iii  despise
iv  defend
v  know a lot about
vi  meet
vii  catch
viii  have nothing else left
ix  reduce
x  finally go to

# 15 Definitions

*Use these verbs and particles to make up phrasal verbs which replace the definitions underlined in the sentences.*

VERBS: brush come do explain go let pick settle stand strip

PARTICLES: away down for into off on out round up without

1 Please be quiet and pay attention, everybody!

2 I'd like to improve my French.

3 Get undressed and wait for the doctor.

4 Do you think there is enough food to feed everybody?

5 I don't think the people will tolerate another increase in taxes.

6 A tall person is always easy to find in a crowd.

7 If we cannot get any bread, we'll just have to manage.

8 All my brother's knives and forks have got "Hotel Excelsior, Cairo" stamped on them. I don't know how he is going to convince people that there is nothing wrong with this situation.

9 Please don't say anything to the children about the party: I want it to be a surprise.

10 I believe that Diana has recently inherited a lot of money.

# 16 Phrasal verbs with two meanings

*Choose a phrasal verb from the list below to complete the captions. Each phrasal verb is used twice but with different meanings. (You may need to change the tense or form of the verb.)*

| blow up | go off | pull up | put back | take off |
|---------|--------|---------|----------|----------|

**1** "Phew! I think this cheese is about to ...................!"

**2** "That's the end of the summer. Time to ....................
.................... the clocks."

**3** "Are you sure you want me to .................... the Coliseum?"

**4** "Be careful how you handle that gun, or it might ................ ................"

**5** "Come on, William, ............. .................. your socks!"

**6** "Please .................. .................. all books in their proper place."

**7** "It's not likely to .................. .................. today, is it?"

**8** " .................. .................. here. I feel like a bite to eat."

**9** "I didn't mean to .................. .................. your balloon as much as that."

**10** "I won't .................. .................. my coat: I'm not staying long."

# 17 Sentence completion

*Choose the phrasal verb which best completes the sentence.*

1   Whole villages have been ................................... by the floods.

   **a**  wiped out   **b**  mopped up   **c**  called off   **d**  run down

2   Stuart is a strange man: I cannot ................... him ................... .

   **a**  make out   **b**  string along   **c**  root out   **d**  spur on

3   It is a serious operation for a woman as old as my grandmother. She's very frail. I hope she ................................... .

   **a**  gets away   **b**  comes round   **c**  pulls through   **d**  stands up

4   It's none of your business: please don't ................................... things that don't concern you.

   **a**  bump into   **b**  meddle with   **c**  tot up   **d**  come across

5   I'm sorry, but I don't think you and I have met before. Are you sure you're not ................... me ................... with somebody else?

   **a**  pairing off   **b**  putting together   **c**  fitting in   **d**  mixing up

6   I'm feeling rather sweaty. Do you mind if I just ................................... a bit before we go out to dinner?

   **a**  tart myself up   **b**  touch myself up   **c**  liven up   **d**  freshen up

7   It's really hard work trying to find the right Mr Smith in the London telephone directory: you may have to ................................... about thirty pages of Smiths.

   **a**  wade through   **b**  rip out   **c**  tramp across   **d**  peer at

8   Ruth wanted to go to Cyprus or Rhodes, her husband Peter wanted to go to Scotland or Ireland. In the end they ................................... Cyprus.

   **a**  hit on   **b**  jumped at   **c**  plumped for   **d**  plunged into

9   The factory is now fully automated, which means that we have been able to ................................... production.

   **a**  run on   **b**  step up   **c**  turn over   **d**  double up

10  I watched a very old professor giving a lecture the other day. He ................... ................... for ages before getting to the point.

   **a**  rambled on   **b**  stumbled forward   **c**  went ahead
   **d**  circled round

# 18 Headlines

*The phrasal verbs in these headlines each contain a one-letter spelling mistake, for instance:* "MAN PRESSED UP AS WOMAN ARRESTED IN PARK", *which should be* "MAN DRESSED UP AS WOMAN ARRESTED IN PARK". *To help you find the mistakes, here is a checklist of the wrong and right letters (given in alphabetical order).*

The wrong letters: A E F L L R S T T X

The right letters: B G L M O P S T U W

1 VICAR "REGRETS SICKING UP HITCHHIKER" ON LONELY ROAD

2 FIRE BRIGADE ON ALERT AS VANDALS THREATEN TO TURN DOWN FARM BUILDINGS

3 LOCAL RESIDENTS PROTEST AS HIPPIES LOVE IN. HIPPIES SAY, "WE HAVE NOWHERE ELSE TO GO"

4 SCIENTISTS TRYING TO FORK OUT MYSTERIES OF HEDGEHOGS' SEX LIVES

5 LATEST TEENAGE CRAZE – SILENT DISCOS – "SPRINTING UP EVERYWHERE"

6 RACE RIOTS: MAYOR APPEARS TO COMMUNITY LEADERS TO CALM DOWN

7 POLICE PRAISE YOUNGSTER WHO JETTED DOWN THIEVES' CAR NUMBER: "COLLECTING CAR NUMBERS IS JUST A HOBBY," SAYS MODEST HERO

8 CRISIS AS PRIME MINISTER RESIGNS: QUEEN LENDS FOR LEADER OF THE OPPOSITION

9 WOMAN IN TEARS AS SHE IS FORCED TO GIVE UP ZOO JOB. "SHE SIMPLY WASN'T CAT OUT FOR THIS KIND OF WORK," SAYS ZOO BOSS

10 MAN AND WIFE SEX OFF ON ROUND-THE-WORLD YACHTING TRIP

# 19 Nouns from phrasal verbs

*Nouns can be formed from phrasal verbs – for instance: "pullover". Choose the correct definition of the following nouns.*

1 A **drawback** is
  a   a disadvantage in a plan
  b   a refund to someone who has paid too much tax
  c   the act of reversing a car round a corner
  d   a sketch of someone done on the back of an envelope

2 **Grown-ups** are
  a   clothes which used to belong to your older brother or sister
  b   mature trees which should be cut down before they fall down
  c   adult people, such as parents
  d   lumps which grow on the backs of people's necks

3 The word **"stopover"** is used to describe
  a   someone who stays too long at a party
  b   a place you stay at to break a long journey
  c   the highest note you can play on a musical instrument
  d   a common stomach problem that people get when they go on holiday

4 A **tip-off** is
  a   something that has fallen off the back of a lorry
  b   information about a crime given to the police
  c   a word to describe the problems of a very short man
  d   the act of raising your hat to a lady

5 The word **"leftovers"** could describe
  a   arm movements in swimming
  b   the remains of a meal
  c   socialists with extremist opinions
  d   girls that nobody wants to dance with

6 A **setback** is
  a   something which happens, such as a delay, to spoil your plans
  b   a house which is a long way from the main road
  c   in chess, returning a piece to the square it came from
  d   a pain caused by standing for a long time in one position

7 A **dropout** is
  a   a person who abandons education or career to lead a different life
  b   a lump of bread or other food which you find on the floor after a messy
      eater has finished a meal
  c   a piece of litter, such as an empty cigarette packet or a sweet wrapper,
      thrown from a moving car
  d   the ugly fold of flesh that hangs over a fat man's belt

8   If you are on **standby**, it means that you
    a   are waiting in a long queue to go to the toilet
    b   are watching other people doing something, such as fighting or playing
        football, without joining in yourself
    c   have been abandoned by your lover, and are hoping to find another
    d   haven't reserved a place on an aeroplane flight but are waiting in case
        there is a spare seat

9   If a man describes a woman as a **"knockout"**, he means that she is
    a   very ugly, the sort that children throw stones at
    b   unfaithful, the sort that goes out with lots of different men
    c   quick-tempered, the sort that is likely to hit you if you annoy her
    d   very attractive, the sort that every man would like to take out

10  A **toss-up** is
    a   the way a bed looks in the morning when you have slept very badly
    b   a way of wishing someone a happy birthday by throwing them up into the
        air
    c   a choice between two equally attractive alternatives
    d   the mark left on the ceiling when someone has tried to turn over an
        omelette in a pan

# 20 Cartoon captions

*Find the right caption for each cartoon.*

a "I wish he'd shut up!"
b "Is this a private fight, or can anyone join in?"
c "Do you think it will clear up later?"
d "Hang on, please!"
e "You should have seen the one that got away!"
f "How nice of you to drop in!"
g "He has slowed down a lot since his operation."
h "Stick 'em up!"
  "Stick what up where?"
i "You can see she takes after her father."
j "I give up. Where have you put my birthday present?"

# 21 Phrasal verbs with GET

*Complete these sentences by adding the correct particle from the list below.*

| | | | | |
|---|---|---|---|---|
| across | back | down | on | through |
| around | behind | in | over | to |
| away | by | into | round | to |

1  "What happened to the television set?"
   "I got .................. with the payments, so they came and took it away."

2  "Where did you get .................. last night? One minute you were dancing, the next minute you had disappeared completely!"

3  Grandma broke her leg, and it was a long time before she was able to get .................. again on her own.

4  "Have you got enough money to live on?"
   "I just manage to get .................. ."

5  Martin was broken-hearted when his wife left him. In fact, I don't think he will ever get .................. it completely.

6  Don't leave your windows open when you are away from home, or a burglar might get .................. .

7  No matter how hard I study, I don't seem to make any progress. It's really beginning to get me .................. .

8  Don't lend money to a friend because you may never get it .................. .

9  This is a lovely pizza, but I don't think I'll get .................. it all.

10  If I can finish these accounts, I'm hoping to get .................. by four o'clock today.

11  He has good ideas, but he's not good at getting them .................. .

12  "Which way to the football stadium?"
    "Turn left when you get .................. the next intersection."

13  "There's not much space for storing things in here. It could be quite a problem."
    "Don't worry, we'll get .................. it somehow."

14  I didn't know what I was getting .................. when I joined the Ecology Party!

15  "How was your interview? How did you get ..................?"
    "I think I got the job."

# 22 Definitions

*Choose the alternative which best matches the meaning of the underlined phrasal verb.*

1  It is snowing heavily at the moment, but it is expected to <u>ease off</u> later.

   **a** get worse   **b** turn to rain   **c** improve   **d** move away

2  You must try not to <u>dwell on</u> your brother's death.

   **a** think too much about   **b** forget   **c** benefit from
   **d** remember

3  John managed to <u>scrape through</u> his final examinations.

   **a** arrive late for   **b** just pass   **c** stay awake during   **d** just fail

4  Mail is <u>piling up</u> at all the main sorting offices because of the postmen's strike.

   **a** not being posted   **b** getting lost   **c** accumulating
   **d** being put into large boxes

5  The war in Lebanon seems to be <u>dragging on.</u>

   **a** coming to an end   **b** involving more and more people
   **c** getting worse   **d** continuing indefinitely

6  I was so late this morning that I hardly had time to <u>gulp down</u> a cup of tea.

   **a** spill   **b** leave unfinished   **c** make myself   **d** drink quickly

7  Why is it that Christopher always <u>wriggles out of</u> doing the washing-up?

   **a** gets paid for   **b** avoids   **c** complains about
   **d** never seems to mind

8  If Sally got up earlier, she wouldn't need to <u>bolt her breakfast down.</u>

   **a** hide her breakfast from the others   **b** eat her breakfast very quickly
   **c** go without breakfast   **d** make her own breakfast

9  The teacher told her students to stop <u>messing about</u>, especially now that their examinations were only two weeks away.

   **a** bringing food into the classroom   **b** coming late all the time
   **c** being absent from class   **d** wasting time

10 I knew that nobody would help me, so I decided to <u>soldier on.</u>

   **a** let someone else do the work   **b** continue by myself
   **c** abandon the job   **d** join the army

# 23 Phrasal verbs with IN

*Complete these sentences by adding the correct verb from the list below. (In some cases, you will need to change the tense or form of the verb.) Use each verb once only.*

| break | call | draw | go | show |
|-------|------|------|------|------|
| bring | deal | get | hand | stay |
| buy | dig | give | keep | trade |

1 He twisted my arm to make me tell what I knew, but I refused to ................... in.

2 "Help yourself! ................... in! There's enough food and drink for everybody!"

3 If you feel like crying, cry. Express your feelings: don't ................... them in.

4 I've decided to ................... in my old car for a new one.

5 We ................... in enough food to last us through the winter.

6 It's quite cold now that the sun's ................... in. Do you really want to go for a swim in the river now?

7 "It's Mr Smith to see you, sir."
   "................... him in!"

8 The days are really ................... in now: it's already dark by five o'clock at this time of year.

9 "You ................... the food in and I'll buy the wine, and we'll have bit of a party."

10 "Has Fred been round to see you lately?"
   "Well, as a matter of fact, he said that he would ................... in today on his way home from work."

11 "Have you done your essay?"
   "Of course! I ................... it in last week."

12 Nowadays, most multinationals ................... in more than one range of products.

13 How on earth did the robbers manage to ................... in without anyone seeing them?

14 "Are you going out tonight?"
   "No, I've got to ................... in and wash my hair."

15 I see they've just ................... in a new law making it illegal for shops to sell cigarettes to children under sixteen.

# 24 Three-part phrasal verbs

*Match each phrasal verb in column A with a word or phrase in column B to give a common phrase. Then find a verb in column C which defines each phrasal verb.*

**Column A**
1  come up to
2  face up to
3  look up to
4  own up to
5  stand up to
6  come up with
7  put up with
8  catch up with
9  keep up with
10  split up with

**Column B**
a  the Joneses
b  your crimes
c  expectations
d  your girl/boy friend
e  noisy neighbours
f  your responsibilities
g  a good idea
h  the car in front
i  a bully
j  someone you respect

**Column C**
i  admit to
ii  reach
iii  accept
iv  leave
v  emulate
vi  fulfil
vii  produce
viii  defy
ix  tolerate
x  admire

# 25 Definitions

*Using the verbs and particles given, make up phrasal verbs which complete the sentences.*

VERBS: come drop fall run show split think throw tip touch

PARTICLES: away down off off on out over round up up

1 To make someone look foolish or to embarrass him in front of other people is to .................... him .................... .

2 To criticise everything that someone does or to tell other people that he is no good is to .................... him .................... .

3 When two lovers have a quarrel, we say that they .................... .................... .

4 If two lovers decide to separate, we say that they .................... .................... .

5 To consider an idea or a suggestion before deciding to accept it is to .................... it .................... .

6 If you happen to mention a subject briefly, we say that you .................... .................... it.

7 When you know that something bad is going to happen, and you warn someone about it, we say that you .................... him .................... .

8 When you regain consciousness after an operation or after fainting, we say that you .................... .................... .

9 When the number of people attending meetings or classes starts to get less, we say that attendance has started to .................... .................... .

10 When you discard something because you no longer need it, you .................... it .................... .

# 26 Phrasal verbs with two meanings

*Each sentence in the first group uses the same phrasal verb as a sentence in the second group. Find the pairs of sentences by putting the following verbs into the sentences. (You may have to change the form or tense of the verb.)*

| break off | cut out | drop in | give away | hang up |
|---|---|---|---|---|
| look into | tear off | turn in | turn round | tuck in |

1   Whenever there was an article in the newspaper about Manchester United, Bill always used to .................... it .................... and paste it in his scrapbook.
2   I don't need all these old clothes. I think I'll just .................... them .................... to our friends.
3   Please .................... .................... and see us any time you are in Bradford.
4   It's getting late: I think I'll .................... .................... .
5   My children are too lazy to open a milk carton with scissors. They just .................... the top .................... .
6   When lovers .................... .................... each other's eyes and say, "I love you," do they really mean it?
7   The two superpowers could not agree on an agenda, so they decided to .................... .................... negotiations.
8   Every night, father goes upstairs to tell the children a story, .................... them .................... and then kisses them goodnight.
9   The company was losing money last year, but this year we have managed to .................... it .................... .
10  (On the telephone) "Please don't .................... .................... until I have had a chance to tell you how sorry I am."

a   The food looked so delicious that we all started to .................... .................... without being asked.
b   The policeman .................... .................... his clothes and dived into the river to save the child.
c   Don't laugh or you'll .................... the game .................... .
d   If you are overweight, it is a good idea to reduce the amount of sugar you eat; in fact, it is better to .................... it .................... completely.
e   Children! Don't throw your coats on the chair. .................... them .................... properly in the wardrobe.
f   When Susan discovered that her boyfriend was a drug-pusher, she decided to .................... him .................... to the police.
g   Some money is missing from the safe. The supervisor has been asked to .................... .................... the matter.
h   What a lovely dress! Please .................... .................... so that I can see the back.
i   Open the box and .................... your money .................... .
j   Please .................... .................... some pieces of chocolate and give them to the children.

# 27 Sentence completion

*Choose the phrasal verb which best completes the sentence.*

1   Charlie had such a bad stomach ache that he was .................. .................... with pain.

    **a** bent down    **b** folded over    **c** doubled up    **d** snapped off

2   Sarah desperately wanted to be an actress, so when they offered her a part in the play, she .................. .................... it.

    **a** burst into    **b** seized on    **c** ran after    **d** jumped at

3   Mrs Milton has forty-three cats. I don't know how she .................. .................... them all.

    **a** looks for    **b** stands by    **c** keeps to    **d** copes with

4   The last item on an agenda is "Any Other Business", which gives people a chance to .................. .................... items that were not dealt with in the main part of the meeting.

    **a** set forth    **b** call out    **c** bring up    **d** hint at

5   If you never put oil in your engine, one day it will .................. .................... .

    **a** seize up    **b** go off    **c** flake out    **d** shut down

6   When the dentist has finished drilling the bad parts from your tooth, he will offer you a glass of peculiar pink liquid and tell you to .................. your mouth .................. .

    **a** brush off    **b** wash up    **c** rinse out    **d** scrub down

7   When the chairman ran off with his secretary, the Board tried to .................. .................... the matter.

    **a** switch off    **b** hush up    **c** calm down    **d** tuck away

8   Unfortunately, somebody spoke to a reporter, and the whole thing .................. .................... .

    **a** poured forth    **b** spilled over    **c** leaked out    **d** splashed down

9   When I got into trouble, all my friends deserted me. My wife was the only person who .................. .................... me.

    **a** stuck by    **b** stood for    **c** held to    **d** leant on

10  Why don't you try praising your students occasionally instead of .................. .................... them all the time?

    **a** crying to    **b** shouting at    **c** rushing into    **d** falling over

# 28 Headlines

*The phrasal verbs in these headlines each contain a one-letter spelling mistake, for instance: "MAN PRESSED UP AS WOMAN ARRESTED IN PARK" which should be "MAN DRESSED UP AS WOMAN ARRESTED IN PARK". To help you find the mistakes, here is a checklist of the wrong and right letters (given in alphabetical order).*

The wrong letters: E F H N N N P T U U

The right letters: A C C H K O R R S T

1  MINISTER PROMISES TO ROOF OUT CORRUPTION IN THE HOUSE OF COMMONS

2  SHOCK MEDICAL REPORT: STUDENTS CRANKING UP UNDER EXAMINATION PRESSURE

3  MISSING YACHT POPE UP UNEXPECTEDLY IN HAWAII

4  FATHER FORCED TO SPELL OUT THOUSANDS TO PAY FOR SON'S MOTORING OFFENCES

5  CHILD BLUNTS OUT TRUTH ABOUT PARENTS' WILD PARTIES

6  HEAVYWEIGHT BOXING CHAMPION REFUSES TO DEFEND TITLE AGAINST YOUNG CHALLENGER: THICKENS OUT AT LAST MOMENT

7  TEACHERS SHIRT ROUND EMBARRASSING ISSUES

8  POLICE MOUNT CAMPAIGN TO STUMP OUT TREE VANDALISM

9  LEADER OF RACIST MOVEMENT TUNES DOWN STATEMENT AFTER MASS PROTESTS

10  YOUNG PRIZEWINNER SAYS SHE WAS SPURNED ON BY HER OLDER SISTER'S EXAMPLE

# 29 Adjectivals from phrasal verbs

*Adjectivals can be made from phrasal verbs, for instance: "an overcast sky", "stick-on soles". Choose the adjectival which completes the phrase beneath each picture, using the following words.*

| VERBS: | cast | drive | get |
|---|---|---|---|
| knock | lean | lock | pick |
| pop | roll | slip | |

| PARTICLES: | away | down | in |
|---|---|---|---|
| off | on | on | to | up | up |
| up | | | |

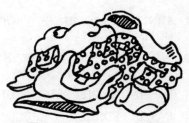

1  This is a ................... truck.

2  This is ................... clothing.

3  These shoes have no laces: they are ................... shoes.

4  This is not an aerosol deodorant: it is a ................... deodorant.

5  The crooks will use this as a ................... vehicle.

**6** There is a sale on: all items are at ................... prices.

**7** This is a ................... book.

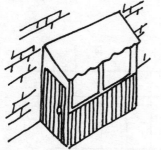

**8** This shed is not free-standing: it is a ................... shed.

**9** The shopowner does not live here: it is a ................... shop.

**10** You can stay in your car: this is a ................... movie.

# 30 Crossword puzzle: "double definitions"

*The answer to each clue is a two-part phrasal verb (or a noun or adjective derived from a phrasal verb). Each clue consists of two parts. The first part gives a dictionary definition; the second gives a typical sentence in which the phrasal verb might be used.*

The following twenty verbs and particles are used:

VERBS: aim book burn carry cast fall lie look set sit stand switch switch touch turn walk work

PARTICLES: about at back back by in off on out out out out over over up up up up

## ACROSS

**3** Be careful; take care (4,3)
"................... ...................! There's a car behind you!"

**5** Point towards (3,2)
"Hold the gun to your shoulder and ................... ................... the target."

**8** The dust which comes from a nuclear explosion (7)
"The trouble with nuclear ................... is that it is radioactive and highly dangerous."

**10** Solve; deduce (4,3)
"Don't ask me what the answer is. Try to ................... it ................... for yourself."

**11** Pay attention; take notice (3,2)
"Then I told him what I *really* thought of him. That made him ................... ................... all right!"

**12** Land (of an aeroplane) (5,4)
"The pilot had radioed ahead that he was having engine trouble, so fire engines were already waiting on the runway for the plane to ................... ................... ."

**16** A kind of railway at an amusement park (10)
"I love the way a ................... railway twists and turns."

**17** The total amount of money taken by a company during the year (8)
"Did you know that the Little Inkling Company more than doubled its ................... last year?"

**18** Become extinguished (4,3)
"We let the fire ................... itself ................... ."

## DOWN

**1** Something you no longer need, especially clothing (4,3)
"Oxfam is always glad to receive ................... ................... clothing."

**2** Wander (4,5)
"The best way to see a town is to park your car and just ................... ................... for an hour or two."

**4** Make a reservation (4,2)
"If you want a ticket for *Hamlet* you really ought to ................... ................... now."

**6** Lipstick, face powder, eye shadow, etc. (6)
"Do you think that men as well as women should use ...................?"

**7** Improve something by adding or removing small details (5,2)

"I haven't got time to repaint the garage door. I think I'll just .................... it .................... here and there."

**9** Stay in bed a bit longer in the morning (3,2)

"Jenny has to get up at six every weekday morning to get the family's breakfast, so she likes to .................... .................... on Sunday mornings."

**11** Change from one thing to another (6,4)

"We have decided to .................... .................... from oil to gas-fired central heating."

**13** Discern; just be able to see (4,3)

"We could only just .................... .................... the farmhouse in the early-morning mist."

**14** Ready and waiting to get a place; go into action, etc. (7)

"On Fridays, all the flights out of Cologne are fully booked, and dozens of people are on .................... ."

**15** Continue (5,2)

"After the police had arrested the man who tried to grab her, the Princess was able to .................... .................... with her tour of inspection."

**16** Organise, establish (3,2)

"The government has .................... .................... a special committee to look into the problem of drug smuggling."

*Complete these sentences by adding the correct particle from the list below.*

| away | for | on | over | through |
|------|------|------|-------|---------|
| by | into | out | round | with |
| down | off | out | round | without |

1 "I hear someone punched John in the face."
"Yes, that's right. The swelling has gone .................., but he's going to have a lovely black eye."

2 I don't think that red blouse really goes ................... your orange skirt, dear.

3 What a lot of people! Do you think there will be enough food to go ...................?

4 The letter was returned to the sender. On the envelope someone had written the words "Gone ................... . No longer at this address".

5 I can't go ................... all the details right now, but I thought you ought to know that your job application has been turned down.

6 What a fascinating story. Do go ...................!

7 There's an awful influenza virus going ................... . I hope you don't catch it.

8 This is a very complex computer program. You might need to go ................... the instructions again before you get the hang of it.

9 Try not to upset Louise, or she's likely to get very angry and go ................... you.

10 "I thought you liked country and western music."
"Well, I used to, but I've really gone ................... it lately."

11 "Good heavens! You're wearing trousers with turnups. I thought they went ................... years ago."
"They did: this is a very, very old suit."

12 Mark was sure that he had picked up his key, but when he went ................... his pockets, he couldn't find it anywhere.

13 Did you know that a camel can go ................... water for thirty days?

14 "Standing on the corner, watching all the girls go ..................." (song).

15 One by one, the street lights went ..................., leaving us in total darkness.

*Choose the alternative which best matches the meaning of the underlined phrasal verb.*

1  It was so hot in the theatre that I almost <u>dropped off.</u>

   **a** decided to leave   **b** fell from the balcony   **c** fainted   **d** fell asleep

2  When the Russian army occupied Belanon, many people refused to <u>knuckle under.</u>

   **a** submit to them   **b** bow down before them   **c** pay their taxes
   **d** shake hands with them

3  Some conference speakers have very little to say, but they are still able to <u>spin out</u> their material.

   **a** change the subject when necessary   **b** remember their words
   **c** make it seem important   **d** make it last a long time

4  As it was getting late, the chairman <u>wound up</u> the meeting.

   **a** postponed   **b** ended   **c** cancelled   **d** timed

5  The boss sometimes lets her typists <u>knock off</u> at four o'clock.

   **a** hand in their work   **b** stop for a tea break   **c** finish work
   **d** meet to make suggestions or complaints about their work

6  As it was my birthday, I decided to <u>lash out on</u> a dinner for all my friends.

   **a** go out for   **b** spend a lot of money on   **c** prepare and cook
   **d** not to provide

7  My dad is always <u>harking back</u> to the time when he was in the army.

   **a** is always complaining about   **b** loves to talk about
   **c** can remember very little about
   **d** likes listening to his friends talking about

8  "What did he say to you?"
   "He told me to <u>clear off.</u>"

   **a** go away   **b** tidy the place up   **c** finish my work
   **d** push the boat into the water

9  I knew exactly what he wanted me to do: he didn't need to <u>spell it out for me.</u>

   **a** tell me how to write it down   **b** help me to do it   **c** explain it any further   **d** plan my life for me

10  Janet is very upset. I'd like you to try and <u>smooth things over</u> if you can.

   **a** tidy the place up for her   **b** calm her down   **c** tell her not to be silly   **d** hide the truth from her

# 33 Phrasal verbs with OFF

*Complete these sentences by adding the correct verb from the list below. (In some cases, you will need to change the tense or form or the verb.) Use each verb once only.*

| | | | | |
|---|---|---|---|---|
| break | fight | hold | ring | sleep |
| call | get | leave | see | slip |
| cut | go | put | send | tip |

1   "Where did you get that fabulous dress?"
    "I saw it in a mail-order catalogue: I had to .................. off for it."

2   I've really .................. off Bill. I though he was such a kind man, but I've found out that he is really very self-centred.

3   The football match had to be .................. off because of rain.

4   I was on the Tube to Victoria, but the train was so crowded that I decided to .................. off at Green Park and walk the rest of the way.

5   The Customs knew all about the drug smugglers because they had been .................. off in advance by a member of the gang.

6   Let's hope the rain will .................. off long enough for them to finish the cricket match.

7   Bill is quite a nice man, but a lot of people are .................. off by his habit of chewing whole cloves of garlic.

8   I've been trying to .................. off a cold all week by taking lots of vitamin C, but I've caught cold anyway.

9   Will you come to the station to .................. me off, or must I go there alone?

10  This is going to be a long meeting, so I suggest that we .................. off now for lunch and resume at two thirty.

11  "Where is everybody?"
    "They're all still in bed, .................. off the effects of last night's party."

12  "As you can see, ladies and gentlemen, the outer casing .................. off easily to allow access to the interior working parts."

13  Whole villages have been .................. off by the heavy flooding following ten days of non-stop rain.

14  When I go to bed, I like to read for about ten minutes. I always turn down the corner of the page when I stop so that, next night, I can pick up exactly where I .................. off.

15  I heard the phone go, but whoever it was had .................. off by the time I got there.

# 34 Three-part phrasal verbs

*Supply the missing particles which follow the verbs in the following captions:*

| back on | back to | behind with | down on | off with |
|---------|---------|-------------|---------|----------|
| on at | out against | out of | out on | up for |

**1** "OK, everybody. Tea break over. Time to get . . . . . . . . . . . . . . . . . . . . . . . . . . . . . . . . . . . . work!"

**2** "This is what happens when you fall . . . . . . . . . . . . . . . . . . . . . . . . . . . . . . . . . . . the rent."

**3** "All right, don't keep going . . . . . . . . . . . . . . . . . . . . . . . . . . . . . . . . . . . . . me. I'll get my hair cut."

**4** "The police have decided to crack . . . . . . . . . . . . . . . . . . . . . . . . . . . . . . . . . . . people who drink and drive."

**5** "My wife has walked .............. ........... me. I can't think why."

**6** "Please don't wait ............... .................... me."

**7** "We speak ................... ................... injustice wherever we find it."

**8** "You know when you look ................... .............. those days, they weren't too bad."

**9** "The problem is that we've run ................... ................... matches.

**10** "And now, ladies and gentlemen, I should like to finish ................... ................... a concerto of my own, which only lasts two hours – or so."

# 35 Definitions

*Using the verbs and particles given, make up phrasal verbs which complete the sentences.*

| VERBS: blow call carry cut fit set shake slip wear work | PARTICLES: down for in off off on out out up up |
|---|---|

1   To make a mistake is to .................. .................... .

2   To leave on a journey is to .................. .................... .

3   To destroy a bridge using explosive is to .................. it .................... .

4   When people demand something, for example, a change in the law, we say that they .................. .................... a change.

5   After a long time and lot of use, things like machines and clothes are no longer any good. We say that in time things .................. .................... .

6   If you decide to reduce the number of cigarettes that you smoke or the amount of food you eat, we say that you have decided to .................. .................... .

7   To solve a problem, such as a mathematical problem, is to .................. it .................... .

8   To continue doing something is to .................. .................... doing it.

9   If you recover easily and quickly from a cold, we say that you were able to .................. it .................... .

10  If new people join an established group and they quickly become accepted, we say that they .................. .................... very well.

# Phrasal verbs with two meanings

*Choose a phrasal verb from the list below to complete the captions. Each phrasal verb is used twice but with different meanings. (You may need to change the tense or form of the verb.)*

| come off | fall out | go out | stand for | switch off |
| --- | --- | --- | --- | --- |

**1** "What do the letters N.U.T. ................................. .............?"

**2** "Don't forget to ..................
.....................the light before you go to bed."

**3** "The artist had tried to give the idea of young love, but I don't think it ....................."

**4** "It looks as if those two have ....................
..................... again."

**5** "He ............... .............. at the same time every night."

**6** "Don't waste your money on getting your hair cut. If you wait long enough it will simply .................... on its own."

**7** "Now, don't let the fire ..................... .............!"

**8** "Are they supposed to ............ .................... like that?"

**9** "That's the third time this week! I'm just not prepared to .................... it any more."

**10** "When he is bored, he simply.................... ...................."

**37** Sentence completion

*Choose the phrasal verb that best completes the sentence.*

1   That's the third time you've asked me where I got the money to buy my car.
    I'm not sure what you're .................. ...................., but I didn't steal the
    money, if that's what you mean.

    **a**  coming to     **b**  working on     **c**  making up     **d**  getting at

2   The crowd was so angry that it took their leaders ages to get them to
    .................. .................... .

    **a**  peter out     **b**  sober up     **c**  simmer down     **d**  whittle away

3   "Is it raining?"
    "Raining? It's absolutely .................. ....................!"

    **a**  pouring down     **b**  streaming away     **c**  spurting out
    **d**  flooding in

4   Do you remember the time that Malcolm panicked when you told him that he
    had woodworm in his concrete patio? He was completely taken in for a while.
    Poor Malcolm! He'll never be able to .................. it .................... .

    **a**  live down     **b**  scratch out     **c**  rip off     **d**  wish away

5   The interrogation seemed to .................. .................... for ages, but in fact it
    only lasted twenty minutes.

    **a**  fritter away     **b**  drag on     **c**  spin off     **d**  play out

6   It's very late and I have a busy day tomorrow. If you don't mind, I think I'll
    .................. .................... now.

    **a**  turn in     **b**  black out     **c**  lay off     **d**  sleep on

7   "That was a very dirty trick you played on your colleagues."
    "I know. I feel badly enough about it as it is. You don't need to ..................
    it .................. ."

    **a**  turn on     **b**  clamp down     **c**  stick up     **d**  rub in

8   Simon never takes anything seriously. He just likes .................. .................... .

    **a**  splashing out     **b**  acting up     **c**  fooling around
    **d**  playing along

9   The business had been allowed to .................. .................... to such an extent
    that it was sold for only a quarter of its true market value.

    **a**  tail off     **b**  fade away     **c**  play out     **d**  run down

10  You may not like what has happened but you cannot simply .................. it
    .................. . It really happened, and you must face up to that fact.

    **a**  dream up     **b**  wish away     **c**  run off     **d**  tone down

# 38 Headlines

*The phrasal verbs in these headlines each contain a one-letter spelling mistake, for instance: "MAN PRESSED UP AS WOMAN ARRESTED IN PARK", which should be "MAN DRESSED UP AS WOMAN ARRESTED IN PARK". To help you find the mistakes, here is a checklist of the wrong and right letters (given in alphabetical order).*

The wrong letters: B F F G L M P R U U

The right letters: A A B C C E F G G T

1 HOUSEWIFE RAMBLES AWAY ALL THE HOUSEKEEPING MONEY AT THE CASINO

2 POLICE SURROUND PRISON AS DANGEROUS CRIMINALS TRY TO FREAK OUT

3 DEMOCRATS PAIN ON REPUBLICANS IN LATEST OPINION POLL

4 SECURITY LIGHTENED UP AT AIRPORTS AS NEW TERRORIST CAMPAIGN BEGINS

5 CONTROVERSY OVER SUNDAY OPENING OF INDIAN SHOPS IN LONDON: SHOPOWNERS SAY THEY INTEND TO CURRY ON AS USUAL

6 VICAR DENIES RUMOURS THAT HE IS LEAVING HIS JOB: "MY PARISHIONERS KNOW THEY CAN MOUNT ON ME TO TAKE CARE OF THEM"

7 NEW ZEALAND NOCTURNAL GROUND PARROT IN DANGER: "WE MUST CONSERVE ITS HABITAT OR IT WILL DIG OUT SOON," SAYS LEADING NATURALIST

8 SEA BREEZES OVER IN COLDEST WINTER IN LIVING MEMORY

9 ANGRY SCENES AS POLICE FLASH WITH STRIKERS

10 CAT, TWENTY-FIVE YEARS OLD, PUSSES AWAY AFTER SHORT ILLNESS

# 39 Nouns from phrasal verbs

*Nouns can be made from phrasal verbs, for instance, "overspill". Complete the following nouns, all of which begin with "out-", using words from the list below. Use each word once only.*

| | | | | |
|---|---|---|---|---|
| break | burst | cast | come | cry |
| fit | lay | let | look | set |

1   A man rejected by his own people is an out.................. .

2   An out.................. of typhoid has been reported.

3   We are still waiting to hear the out.................. of the government inquiry into the rail disaster.

4   There has been a huge public out.................. against the proposal to demolish the village church.

5   "And now the weather forecast. Today, there will be rain everywhere. The out.................. for the weekend: more rain."

6   Suddenly, Sue lost her temper and started screaming and swearing. Everyone was shocked by her out.................. .

7   Everyone knew from the out.................. that the plan would not work.

8   I decided to treat myself to a new out.................., including new shoes, to go on holiday.

9   Apart from the initial out.................. on equipment, it cost us very little to set up our business.

10  A shop is a retail out.................. for manufactured goods.

# 40 Word square

Find these words in the word square. We have done the first one to help you.
Please note that the words may be horizontal, vertical or diagonal, and that
they may be written backwards or forwards.

| | | |
|---|---|---|
| COVER UP | MAKE UP | SET UP |
| HAND OUT | MIX UP | SHOW DOWN |
| HANG OVER | OUT LOOK | SIT IN |
| HIDE AWAY | PICK UP | TEAR AWAY |
| LEAN TO | PIN UP | TRADE OFF |
| LINK UP | SELL OUT | WARM UP |
| LOOK IN | SET BACK | |

```
S  H  O  W  D  O  W  N  A  E  S

E  F  F  O  E  D  A  R  T  U  Y

T  S  I  T  I  N  R  E  F  T  O

B  N  R  N  O  P  M  I  X  U  P

A  L  E  A  T  O  U  L  L  E  S

C  O  V  E  R  U  P  K  R  P  E

K  O  O  L  T  U  O  K  C  O  T

R  K  G  M  E  N  P  D  W  I  U

L  I  N  K  U  P  P  I  N  U  P

E  N  A  T  E  A  R  A  W  A  Y

T  M  H  Y  A  W  A  E  D  I  H
```

# Phrasal verbs with BE

*Complete these sentences by adding the correct particle from the list below. Use each word once only.*

| about | away | from | off | through |
|-------|------|------|-----|---------|
| after | back | like | on | up |
| around | for | into | over | with |

1  "Haven't you finished yet?"
   "Don't worry, I'm nearly ................... ."

2  "Please hurry up!"
   "OK, I'll be ................... you in just a second."

3  "Is the boss in?"
   "No, I'm afraid he's ................... on leave at the moment."

4  "When will he be ...................?"
   "Not until next Wednesday."

5  "What a complicated instrument panel! What's this red button ...................?"
   "It's the ejector seat. Please don't press –"

6  "Shall we watch some television?"
   "If you like. What's ...................?"

7  "What's ...................? You look as if you had seen a ghost!"
   "Who said that?"

8  It's getting late. I'd better be ................... before my father sends out a search party.

9  "What's the book?"
   "It's a novel called *Moby Dick*."
   "What's it ...................?"
   "Whales."

10  The traffic was so bad that by the time we got to the theatre, the concert was almost ................... .

11  "I'm a bit busy at the moment, but I'd love to have a chat with you. Will you be ................... for a while yet?"
   "Oh, yes, I shan't leave much before six o'clock."

12  Robert is for ever changing his hobby. Last year it was birdwatching. Now, he's really ................... stamp collecting.

13  "That's the third time this week that Ruth has phoned me. I wonder what she's ................... ."

14  "Where are you ...................?"
   "Birmingham."

15  "What is Birmingham ...................?"
   "I don't know. I left there when I was three months old, and I've never been there since."

# 42 Definitions

*Choose the alternative which best matches the meaning of the underlined phrase.*

1  Simon hasn't got a job, and isn't trying to get one: he just <u>sponges on</u> his friends.

   a  works with them      b  complains to them about his situation
   c  borrows money from them      d  takes advantage of their kindness

2  The London-to-Sydney flight <u>touched down</u> in Bombay.

   a  made a stop      b  crashed      c  flew low      d  was forced to land

3  Jeremy loves <u>tinkering with</u> old sports cars.

   a  impressing girls by taking them out in      b  driving fast in
   c  buying and selling      d  trying to repair

4  The doctor is busy right now, but she could probably <u>fit</u> you <u>in</u> later.

   a  examine      b  try to cure      c  find time to see      d  look after

5  At first, the managing director insisted that he was right and everyone else was mistaken, but in the end he was forced to <u>climb down.</u>

   a  apologise      b  admit that he was wrong      c  join in the discussion
   d  resign as managing director

6  "May I ask you a question?"
   "<u>Fire away!</u>"

   a  Don't worry! There's no danger.      b  No!      c  Go ahead!
   d  Please leave me alone!

7  In London this morning, three men wearing masks <u>held up</u> a van carrying gold bullion.

   a  robbed      b  lifted      c  delayed      d  stole

8  Rioting in Beirut was <u>sparked off</u> by the arrest of one of the Druze community leaders.

   a  prevented      b  caused      c  delayed      d  exploded

9  Tell me, Sir Walter, what made you <u>hit upon</u> the idea of putting tobacco up your nose?

   a  finally reject      b  suddenly think of      c  openly criticise
   d  carefully develop

10  I was not a success as a door-to-door salesman. The first house I went to, a lady opened the door and told me to <u>buzz off.</u>

   a  stop ringing the doorbell      b  shut up
   c  try to be more interesting      d  go away and leave her alone

# 43 Phrasal verbs with OUT

*Complete these sentences by adding the correct verb from the list below. (In some cases, you will need to change the tense or form of the verb.) Use each verb once only.*

| | | | | |
|---|---|---|---|---|
| dig | fall | pick | slip | throw |
| drop | help | rub | stand | wipe |
| dry | pass | show | take | work |

1 Don always uses a pencil when he is writing a report, so that, if he decides to remove something from it, he can just .................. it out.

2 "Where's Jonathan?"
"He won't be long. He's just .................. out to the tobacconist's to get some cigarettes."

3 The idea of an identity parade is quite simple. You stand a number of people in a line, including the suspected person. Then a witness is asked to .................. out the suspect from the others.

4 There has been no rain at all this summer: even the village pond has .................. out completely.

5 To celebrate my examination success, my parents .................. me out for dinner.

6 It looks as if Diana and her husband have .................. out again: they're not speaking to each other.

7 "Do you like my new pink suit with the large blue spots on it?"
"Well, it certainly makes you .................. out from the crowd."

8 Mr Kafka could never have found his way out of the building by himself, so it was a good thing that the boss's secretary offered to .................. him out.

9 The fighting outside Maputo has been the heaviest of the war, and it is known that one army division has been completely .................. out.

10 "I hear that you and Vivienne have split up. What happened?"
"Well, we tried to make a go of it, but things just didn't .................. out as we had hoped."

11 Justine is doing voluntary work in her spare time: she is .................. out at the old people's home in Winton.

12 I need some information about American football. Please could you look in the file and .................. out all the newspaper articles you can find?

13 After the first year, very few students .................. out: most go on to complete their studies.

14 "Do you really want all these old magazines or can I .................. them out?"
"No, don't do that. I might want to look at them again one day."

15 Some people are so nervous that they .................. out at the sight of blood.

# 44 Three-part phrasal verbs

*Supply the missing particles which follow the verbs in the following captions.*

| away with | down to | forward to | off for | on about |
|---|---|---|---|---|
| out for | out of | out of | out on | up on |

**1** "SEND........................ YOUR COPY TODAY! ONLY TWENTY-FIVE DOLLARS."

**2** "He's been dining ........................ the story every since!"

**3** "He's decided to opt ........................ normal society and go back to his job in the city."

**4** "What it really boils ........................ then, is that you don't love me any more. Is that it?"

**5** "Stay wide awake, Perkins. The enemy can sneak . . . . . . . . . . . . . . . . . . . . . . . . . . . . . you and have you before you can say 'Jack Robinson'!"

**6** "You'll never get . . . . . . . . . . . . . . . . . . . . . . . . . . . . . it!"

**7** "Don't worry, he's just a puppy. He'll soon grow . . . . . . . . . . . . . . . . . . . . . . . . . . . . . . . . . it."

**8** Not everyone looks . . . . . . . . . . . . . . . . . . . . . . . . . . . . . Christmas.

**9** "Don't accept the first offer you get: stick . . . . . . . . . . . . . . . . . . . . . . . . . . . . the price you want."

**10** "It's no good going . . . . . . . . . . . . . . . . . . . . . . . . . . . . . it. You lost, and that's all there is to it."

# 45 Definitions

*Using the verbs and particles given, make up phrasal verbs which complete the sentences. (In some cases, you will need to change the tense or form of the verb.)*

VERBS: drop get give hang look play pull put show turn

PARTICLES: about away down in off off out through up up

1 I just .................. .................... to wish you a Merry Christmas.

2 John is not very punctual. He usually .................. .................... ten minutes after the lesson has started.

3 After the accident at the nuclear power station, the authorities tried to .................. .................... the danger to the public from radioactive waste.

4 Switzerland had intended to enter a team for the International Tiddlywinks Contest, but had to .................. .................... at the last moment when they realised that nobody in Switzerland knew how to play the game.

5 The Parish Council meeting which was scheduled for the 12th has been .................. .................... until the 26th to give the chairman time to sharpen his pencil.

6 Robert Brent has .................. .................... his attempt to beat the hard-boiled egg eating record because he is afraid of getting salmonella.

7 Several people .................. .................... the draft report, but there were still a number of spelling mistakes in the final version.

8 The police chased the thieves for several miles but they managed to .................. .................... because their car was faster than the policemen's bicycles.

9 Don't take any notice of Ruth. She always .................. .................... whenever we have visitors.

10 There's nothing for youngsters to do in Hadley except .................. .................... on street corners, chatting and smoking and hoping for something interesting to happen.

# 46 Phrasal verbs with two meanings

*Each sentence in the first group uses the same phrasal verb as a sentence in the second group. Find the pairs of sentences by putting the following verbs into the sentences. (In some cases, you may need to change the tense or form of the verb.)*

---

bump into   clear up   cover up   cut down   leak out   let off   look over
play at   set off   stand by

---

1   He should have gone to prison but the judge .................. him ..................
    with a caution.

2   I .................. .................. what I said: I refuse to take back a word of it.

3   There is a wonderful view from our back window because we ..................
    .................. the golf course.

4   It's raining quite heavily at the moment, but I hope it will ..................
    .................. later in time for the barbecue.

5   There used to be a lovely old oak tree in the garden, but it became so
    dangerous that we decided to .................. it .................. .

6   In Muslim countries women tourists are advised to wear long dresses with
    long sleeves in order to .................. .................. their bare arms and legs.

7   I happened to .................. .................. Kate the other day; I hadn't seen her
    for ages.

8   We decided to .................. .................. early in order to avoid the morning
    traffic jams.

9   What do you think you're .................. ..................? Stop that at once!

10  No matter how hard you try to keep a secret, it always ..................
    .................. sooner or later.

---

a   The bright colours of the roses were .................. .................. by the soft yellow
    brick of the garden wall.

b   There was a hole in the bottom of the flask, and all the liquid ..................
    .................. .

c   Although it seemed just the house we wanted, we decided to ..................
    .................. it very carefully before making up our minds to buy it.

d   It is very dangerous to .................. .................. fireworks when holding them
    in your hand.

e   After a party, do you .................. .................. the mess right away, or do you
    leave it until the next morning?

f   The children were in the garden .................. .................. cowboys and Indians.

59

**g**  A large lady with an even larger shopping basket .................. .................... me the other day, and practically knocked me over.

**h**  You really ought to stop smoking, but if you can't, then you should at least try to .................. .................... to no more than ten a day.

**i**  A woman was attacked in the street. Instead of going to help her, other people just .................. .................... and watched. Isn't that terrible?

**j**  The Nixon administration tried to .................. .................... the truth about Watergate, but two journalists managed to find out what had really happened.

# Sentence completion

*In sentences 1 to 5, three of the four verbs are correct, and all mean more or less the same thing. The other one does not fit, either because it means something different or because it is not used with the particles which follow. Find the ones that don't fit in sentences 1 to 5, then use them to complete sentences a to e.*

1   My father doesn't approve of the people I   go     around with.
                                              hang
                                              play
                                              knock

2   When people panic, they usually   lash     out at the nearest person.
                                      strike
                                      hit
                                      rush

3   Don't decide too quickly;   hold     out for the result you want.
                              stick
                              shell
                              hang

4   If you're not careful, you'll   stock     up with a face like mine.
                                 end
                                 land
                                 finish

5   "Why don't you come round to our place for a drink one night?"
    "I tell you what, I'll   butt    in on you on the way home tomorrow."
                          drop
                          look
                          call

a   I've had to ................... out for four new tyres on my car.

b   I didn't mean to ................... in on your conversation, but I couldn't help overhearing my name mentioned.

c   When the popstar left the theatre all his fans ................... at him.

d   I was just ................... around with this gun when it went off. Luckily, nobody was hurt.

e   Are you expecting bad weather? Do you always ................... up with enough food to last you six months?

# 48 Headlines

*The phrasal verbs in these headlines each contain a one-letter spelling mistake, for instance:* "MAN PRESSED UP AS WOMAN ARRESTED IN PARK", *which should be* "MAN DRESSED UP AS WOMAN ARRESTED IN PARK". *To help you find the mistakes, here is a checklist of the wrong and right letters (given in alphabetical order).*

The wrong letters: A C J L M R R T T W

The right letters:   B H L O P P T T W W

1 NEW TEAM SHARING UP WELL. "SHOULD WIN THE CUP," SAYS TRAINER

2 DON'T KNACK OFF EARLY ON FRIDAY AFTERNOONS, WORKERS WARNED

3 YOUNGSTERS LUCK IN AT VILLAGE FEAST

4 OLD PEOPLE ADVISED TO TRAP UP WELL DURING COLD SPELL

5 ANGRY SCENES IN CONGRESS: PRESIDENT WASHES OUT AT OPPOSITION'S "DISHONEST TACTICS"

6 UNWANTED AND UNLOVED: VILLAGERS TELL GYPSIES, "STOVE OFF AND LEAVE US ALONE"

7 AFTER FIFTEEN YEARS, HUSBAND FINALLY MUMBLES TO WIFE'S LOVER

8 MANCHESTER MAN JUMPS INTO LONG-LOST BROTHER IN NEW YORK NIGHTCLUB

9 OFFICIALS CRITICISED FOR SCANNING ABOUT IN EXPENSIVE CARS AT TAXPAYERS' EXPENSE

10 WHOLE TRIBES WIRED OUT BY INFLUENZA EPIDEMIC

# 49 Adjectivals from phrasal verbs

*Adjectivals can be made from phrasal verbs, for instance, "an overcast sky", "stick-on soles". Choose the adjectival which completes the sentence.*

1 Outside the town, the speed limit is 70 mph. In .................. areas, the speed limit is reduced to 30 mph.

   **a** made-up   **b** packed-up   **c** built-up   **d** filled-in

2 An industrial society which makes goods that are not designed to last is known as a .................. society.

   **a** fallout   **b** takeaway   **c** set-aside   **d** throwaway

3 A neglected part of a city is called a .................. area.

   **a** washed-out   **b** left-over   **c** cast-off   **d** run-down

4 Someone who is mentally confused can be described as a .................. person.

   **a** cast-off   **b** mixed-up   **c** patched-up   **d** broken-down

5 When you are really tired after working hard, you can say that you are .................. .

   **a** dried up   **b** worn out   **c** written off   **d** laid back

6 If you think and behave as if you were better than everyone else, people may describe you as .................. .

   **a** wound up   **b** dressed up   **c** pop up   **d** stuck up

7 After a lesson or a course, the teacher may give you additional tasks to do. These are known as .................. activities.

   **a** follow-up   **b** stick-on   **c** work-out   **d** stand-by

8 A blouse that is transparent is called a .................. blouse.

   **a** look-in   **b** peep-show   **c** off-beat   **d** see-through

9 When one company tries to gain control of another by offering a high price for its shares, it is making a .................. bid.

   **a** breakthrough   **b** showdown   **c** makeup   **d** takeover

10 A person who is rather reserved or cold in behaviour can be described as .................. .

   **a** stand offish   **b** carried away   **c** overdrawn   **d** outcast

# 50 Proverbs

*Here are ten well-known proverbs or expressions containing phrasal verbs.
Choose from this list the phrasal verb which fits in each expression (you may
need to change the tense or form of the verb).*

| bite off | come out | cut off | look after | pick up |
|----------|----------|---------|------------|---------|
| put off | run away | throw out | turn over | wait for |

1  If you always try to do too much, people may say, "Don't .................. more
    than you can chew."

2  Sometimes, in a bad situation, there may still be some good things. Try not to
    ".................. .................. the baby with the bath water".

3  If somebody has behaved badly in the past but promises to be good in future,
    we say he has promised to ".................. .................. a new leaf".

4  If you try to hurt someone else, but you can only do it by causing even bigger
    problems for yourself, we say that you have ".................. .................. your
    nose to spite your face".

5  The advice not to postpone work that should be done now is expressed in the
    saying: "Never .................. .................. till tomorrow what you can do today."

6  Time, like the tide (the rising and falling of the sea), goes on whether we like
    it or not: "Time and tide .................. .................. no man."

7  If you are an optimist and believe that things always get better eventually,
    you might say, "The sun always .................. .................. after the rain."

8  "He who fights and .................. ..................
    Lives to fight another day."

9  If you are careful with money, even small amounts, you will be better off:
    ".................. .................. the pennies and the pounds will ..................
    .................. themselves." (The same verb is used twice.)

10  "See a pin and .................. it ..................
    And all day long you'll have good luck.
    See a pin and let it lie –
    You'll need that pin before you die."

# Answers

## TEST 1

| | | | | | |
|---|---|---|---|---|---|
| 1 | comes before | 6 | come out | 11 | come along |
| 2 | come in | 7 | came forward | 12 | come into |
| 3 | come back | 8 | come from | 13 | comes up |
| 4 | came across | 9 | coming to | 14 | comes off |
| 5 | come round | 10 | come on | 15 | come about |

## TEST 2

| | | | | | | |
|---|---|---|---|---|---|---|
| 1 | a | cover my expenses | 6 | a | reluctantly pay |
| 2 | b | go to bed | 7 | c | take money from |
| 3 | d | settled their differences | 8 | c | go with them |
| 4 | b | fell asleep | 9 | a | reprimanded me |
| 5 | a | go to several different shops to compare prices | 10 | a | forgot what I wanted to say |

## TEST 3

| | | | | | |
|---|---|---|---|---|---|
| 1 | stay away | 6 | fade away | 11 | drove away |
| 2 | break away | 7 | keep children away | 12 | look away |
| 3 | slipped away | 8 | take away | 13 | tucked away |
| 4 | running away | 9 | threw them away | 14 | sent him away |
| 5 | tow it away | 10 | give them away | 15 | passed away |

## TEST 4

| | | | | | |
|---|---|---|---|---|---|
| 1 | d | vii | 6 | b | v |
| 2 | f | ix | 7 | j | i |
| 3 | a | iii | 8 | g | x |
| 4 | i | ii | 9 | c | iv |
| 5 | h | viii | 10 | e | vi |

## TEST 5

| | | | | | |
|---|---|---|---|---|---|
| 1 | give away | 5 | clear up | 8 | fill in |
| 2 | step up | 6 | draw up | 9 | put forward |
| 3 | carry out | 7 | make one up | 10 | turn down |
| 4 | break off | | | | |

## TEST 6

| | | | | |
|---|---|---|---|---|
| 1 and g | fall through | 6 and f | see through |
| 2 and d | dry up | 7 and i | fall off |
| 3 and j | put off | 8 and h | take back |
| 4 and b | make up | 9 and e | run across |
| 5 and a | look up | 10 and c | catch on |

## TEST 7

| | | | | | | |
|---|---|---|---|---|---|---|
| 1 | a | flaked out | 6 | c | skate over |
| 2 | c | crop up | 7 | d | size up |
| 3 | b | sound out | 8 | a | shrug off |
| 4 | a | blends in | 9 | d | snapped up |
| 5 | d | Roll on | 10 | a | dawned on |

## TEST 8

| | | | | |
|---|---|---|---|---|
| 1 | lay off | 6 | locked up |
| 2 | pining for | 7 | try for |
| 3 | torn between | 8 | sums up |
| 4 | hints at | 9 | washing up |
| 5 | adds to | 10 | nodding off |

## TEST 9

| | | | | |
|---|---|---|---|---|
| 1 | breakdown | 6 | checkout |
| 2 | breakthrough | 7 | takeaway |
| 3 | write-off | 8 | turnout |
| 4 | tailback | 9 | hold-up |
| 5 | layby | 10 | hangover |

## TEST 10

### Across

| | | | | |
|---|---|---|---|---|
| 1 | come down | 10 | bowl over |
| 4 | send off | 13 | down |
| 7 | outbreak | 14 | on |
| 8 | do | 15 | string |

### Down

| | | | | |
|---|---|---|---|---|
| 1 | cast-off | 9 | own |
| 2 | end | 10 | book |
| 3 | offset | 11 | out |
| 5 | note down | 12 | run |
| 6 | skate | 16 | in |

## TEST 11

| | | | | | | |
|---|---|---|---|---|---|---|
| 1 | taken over | 6 | taken off | 11 | take after |
| 2 | take up | 7 | take (me) for | 12 | taken (too much) on |
| 3 | taken to | 8 | taken in | 13 | take (it) in |
| 4 | taken down | 9 | take (it) back | 14 | take (them all) back |
| 5 | take out | 10 | take (it) up | 15 | taken to |

## TEST 12

| | | | | | |
|---|---|---|---|---|---|
| 1 | d | keep going | 6 | b | find |
| 2 | b | leave at once | 7 | d | depend on her to do it |
| 3 | a | interrupt you | 8 | d | glibly produces |
| 4 | c | encouraged me | 9 | c | decorated |
| 5 | a | left in a hurry | 10 | c | very tired and pale |

## TEST 13

| | | | | | |
|---|---|---|---|---|---|
| 1 | step down | 6 | tracked (him) down | 11 | let (you) down |
| 2 | turned (me) down | 7 | broke down | 12 | lie down |
| 3 | shut down | 8 | put (it) down | 13 | settled down |
| 4 | keep down | 9 | taken down | 14 | burnt (or burned) (it) down |
| 5 | cut down | 10 | worn down | 15 | shouting (him) down |

## TEST 14

| | | | | | |
|---|---|---|---|---|---|
| 1 | i | vii | 6 | b | v |
| 2 | d | ix | 7 | h | i |
| 3 | a | iii | 8 | f | x |
| 4 | j | ii | 9 | e | iv |
| 5 | g | viii | 10 | c | vi |

## TEST 15

| | | | | | |
|---|---|---|---|---|---|
| 1 | settle down | 5 | stand for | 8 | explain away |
| 2 | brush up | 6 | pick out | 9 | let on |
| 3 | strip off | 7 | do without | 10 | come into |
| 4 | go round | | | | |

## TEST 16

| | |
|---|---|
| 1 and 4 | go off |
| 2 and 6 | put back |
| 3 and 9 | blow up |
| 5 and 8 | pull up |
| 7 and 10 | take off |

## TEST 17

| | | | | | |
|---|---|---|---|---|---|
| 1 | a | wiped out | 6 | d | freshen up |
| 2 | a | make him out | 7 | a | wade through |
| 3 | c | pulls through | 8 | c | plumped for |
| 4 | b | meddle with | 9 | b | step up |
| 5 | d | mixing me up | 10 | a | rambled on |

## TEST 18

| | | | |
|---|---|---|---|
| 1 | picking up | 6 | appeals to |
| 2 | burn down | 7 | jotted down |
| 3 | move in | 8 | sends for |
| 4 | work out | 9 | cut out |
| 5 | springing up | 10 | set off |

## TEST 19

| | | | | | |
|---|---|---|---|---|---|
| 1 | a | 5 | b | 8 | d |
| 2 | c | 6 | a | 9 | d |
| 3 | b | 7 | a | 10 | c |
| 4 | b | | | | |

## TEST 20

| | | | | | |
|---|---|---|---|---|---|
| 1 | h | 5 | c | 8 | j |
| 2 | d | 6 | f | 9 | i |
| 3 | g | 7 | a | 10 | e |
| 4 | b | | | | |

## TEST 21

| | | | | | |
|---|---|---|---|---|---|
| 1 | got behind | 6 | get in | 11 | getting (them) across |
| 2 | get to | 7 | get (me) down | 12 | get to |
| 3 | get around | 8 | get (it) back | 13 | get round |
| 4 | get by | 9 | get through | 14 | getting into |
| 5 | get over | 10 | get away | 15 | get on |

## TEST 22

| | | | | | | |
|---|---|---|---|---|---|---|
| 1 | c | improve | 6 | d | drink quickly |
| 2 | a | think too much about | 7 | b | avoids |
| 3 | b | just pass | 8 | b | eat her breakfast very quickly |
| 4 | c | accumulating | 9 | d | wasting time |
| 5 | d | continuing indefinitely | 10 | b | continue by myself |

## TEST 23

| | | | | | |
|---|---|---|---|---|---|
| 1 | give in | 6 | gone in | 11 | handed (it) in |
| 2 | Dig in! | 7 | Show (him) in | 12 | deal in |
| 3 | keep (them) in | 8 | drawing in | 13 | break in |
| 4 | trade in | 9 | get (the food) in | 14 | stay in |
| 5 | bought in | 10 | call in | 15 | brought in |

## TEST 24

| | | | | | | | |
|---|---|---|---|---|---|---|---|
| 1 | c | vi | 6 | g | vii |
| 2 | f | iii | 7 | e | ix |
| 3 | j | x | 8 | h | ii |
| 4 | b | i | 9 | a | v |
| 5 | i | viii | 10 | d | iv |

## TEST 25

| | | | | |
|---|---|---|---|---|
| 1 | show (him) up | 6 | touch on (it) |
| 2 | run (him) down | 7 | tip (him) off |
| 3 | fall out | 8 | come round |
| 4 | split up | 9 | drop off |
| 5 | think (it) over | 10 | throw (it) away |

## TEST 26

| | | | | |
|---|---|---|---|---|
| 1 and d | cut out | 6 and g | look into |
| 2 and c | give away | 7 and j | break off |
| 3 and i | drop in | 8 and a | tuck in |
| 4 and f | turn in | 9 and h | turn round |
| 5 and b | tear off | 10 and e | hang up |

**TEST 27**

| | | | | | | |
|---|---|---|---|---|---|---|
| 1 | c | doubled up | 6 | c | rinse out |
| 2 | d | jumped at | 7 | b | hush up |
| 3 | d | copes with | 8 | c | leaked out |
| 4 | c | bring up | 9 | a | stuck by |
| 5 | a | seize up | 10 | b | shouting at |

**TEST 28**

| | | | | |
|---|---|---|---|---|
| 1 | root out | 6 | chickens out |
| 2 | cracking up | 7 | skirt round |
| 3 | pops up | 8 | stamp out |
| 4 | shell out | 9 | tones down |
| 5 | blurts out | 10 | spurred on |

**TEST 29**

| | | | | |
|---|---|---|---|---|
| 1 | pick-up | 6 | knockdown |
| 2 | cast-off | 7 | pop-up |
| 3 | slip-on | 8 | lean-to |
| 4 | roll-on | 9 | lock-up |
| 5 | getaway | 10 | drive-in |

**TEST 30**

**Across**

| | | | | |
|---|---|---|---|---|
| 3 | look out | 12 | touch down |
| 5 | aim at | 16 | switchback |
| 8 | fallout | 17 | turnover |
| 10 | work out | 18 | burn out |
| 11 | sit up | | |

**Down**

| | | | | |
|---|---|---|---|---|
| 1 | cast off | 11 | switch over |
| 2 | walk about | 13 | make out |
| 4 | book up | 14 | standby |
| 6 | makeup | 15 | carry on |
| 7 | touch up | 16 | set up |
| 9 | lie in | | |

**TEST 31**

| | | | | | | |
|---|---|---|---|---|---|---|
| 1 | gone down | 6 | go on | 11 | went out |
| 2 | goes with | 7 | going round | 12 | went through |
| 3 | go round | 8 | go over | 13 | go without |
| 4 | gone away | 9 | go for | 14 | go by |
| 5 | go into | 10 | gone off | 15 | went out |

**TEST 32**

| | | | | | | |
|---|---|---|---|---|---|---|
| 1 | d | fell asleep | 6 | b | spend a lot of money |
| 2 | a | submit to them | 7 | b | loves to talk about |
| 3 | d | make it last a long time | 8 | a | go away |
| 4 | b | ended | 9 | c | explain it any further |
| 5 | c | finish work | 10 | b | calm her down |

## TEST 33

| | | | | | |
|---|---|---|---|---|---|
| 1 | send off | 6 | hold off | 11 | sleeping off |
| 2 | gone off | 7 | put off | 12 | slips off |
| 3 | called off | 8 | fight off | 13 | cut off |
| 4 | get off | 9 | see (me) off | 14 | left off |
| 5 | tipped off | 10 | break off | 15 | rung off |

## TEST 34

| | | | |
|---|---|---|---|
| 1 | get back to | 6 | wait up for |
| 2 | fall behind with | 7 | speak out against |
| 3 | going on at | 8 | look back on |
| 4 | crack down on | 9 | run out of |
| 5 | walked out on | 10 | finish off with |

## TEST 35

| | | | |
|---|---|---|---|
| 1 | slip up | 6 | cut down |
| 2 | set off | 7 | work (it) out |
| 3 | blow (it) up | 8 | carry on |
| 4 | call for | 9 | shake (it) off |
| 5 | wear out | 10 | fit in |

## TEST 36

| | |
|---|---|
| 1 and 9 | stand for |
| 2 and 10 | switch off |
| 3 and 8 | come off |
| 4 and 6 | fall out |
| 5 and 7 | go out |

## TEST 37

| | | | | | | |
|---|---|---|---|---|---|---|
| 1 | d | getting at | 6 | a | turn in |
| 2 | c | simmer down | 7 | d | rub (it) in |
| 3 | a | pouring down | 8 | c | fooling around |
| 4 | a | live (it) down | 9 | d | run down |
| 5 | b | drag on | 10 | b | wish (it) away |

## TEST 38

| | | | |
|---|---|---|---|
| 1 | gambles away | 6 | count on |
| 2 | break out | 7 | die out |
| 3 | gain on | 8 | freezes over |
| 4 | tightened up | 9 | clash with |
| 5 | carry on | 10 | passes away |

## TEST 39

| | | | |
|---|---|---|---|
| 1 | outcast | 6 | outburst |
| 2 | outbreak | 7 | outset |
| 3 | outcome | 8 | outfit |
| 4 | outcry | 9 | outlay |
| 5 | outlook | 10 | outlet |

**TEST 40**

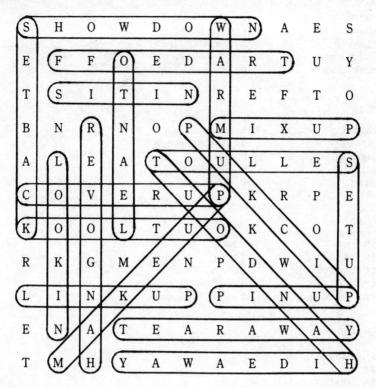

| S | H | O | W | D | O | W | N | A | E | S |
|---|---|---|---|---|---|---|---|---|---|---|
| E | F | F | O | E | D | A | R | T | U | Y |
| T | S | I | T | I | N | R | E | F | T | O |
| B | N | R | N | O | P | M | I | X | U | P |
| A | L | E | A | T | O | U | L | L | E | S |
| C | O | V | E | R | U | P | K | R | P | E |
| K | O | O | L | T | U | O | K | C | O | T |
| R | K | G | M | E | N | P | D | W | I | U |
| L | I | N | K | U | P | P | I | N | U | P |
| E | N | A | T | E | A | R | A | W | A | Y |
| T | M | H | Y | A | W | A | E | D | I | H |

**TEST 41**

| | | | | | | | | |
|---|---|---|---|---|---|---|---|---|
| 1 | through | 6 | on | 11 | around |
| 2 | with | 7 | up | 12 | into |
| 3 | away | 8 | off | 13 | after |
| 4 | back | 9 | about | 14 | from |
| 5 | for | 10 | over | 15 | like |

**TEST 42**

| | | | | | | |
|---|---|---|---|---|---|---|
| 1 | c | borrows money from them | 6 | c | Go ahead! |
| 2 | a | made a stop | 7 | a | robbed |
| 3 | d | trying to repair | 8 | b | caused |
| 4 | c | find time to see | 9 | b | suddenly think of |
| 5 | b | admit that he was wrong | 10 | d | go away and leave her alone |

**TEST 43**

| | | | | | |
|---|---|---|---|---|---|
| 1 | rub (it) out | 6 | fallen out | 11 | helping out |
| 2 | slipped out | 7 | stand out | 12 | dig out |
| 3 | pick out | 8 | show (him) out | 13 | drop out |
| 4 | dried out | 9 | wiped out | 14 | throw (them) out |
| 5 | took (me) out | 10 | work out | 15 | pass out |

## TEST 44

| | | | |
|---|---|---|---|
| 1 | send off for | 6 | get away with |
| 2 | dining out on | 7 | grow out of |
| 3 | opt out of | 8 | looks forward to |
| 4 | boils down to | 9 | stick out for |
| 5 | sneak up on | 10 | going on about |

## TEST 45

| | | | |
|---|---|---|---|
| 1 | dropped in | 6 | given up |
| 2 | turns up | 7 | looked through |
| 3 | play down | 8 | get away |
| 4 | pull out | 9 | · shows off |
| 5 | put off | 10 | hanging about |

## TEST 46

| | | | |
|---|---|---|---|
| 1 and **d** | let off | 6 and **j** | cover up |
| 2 and **i** | stand by | 7 and **g** | bump into |
| 3 and **c** | look over | 8 and **a** | set off |
| 4 and **e** | clear up | 9 and **f** | play at |
| 5 and **h** | cut down | 10 and **b** | leak out |

## TEST 47

| | |
|---|---|
| 1 and **d** | play |
| 2 and **c** | rush |
| 3 and **a** | shell |
| 4 and **e** | stock |
| 5 and **b** | butt |

## TEST 48

| | | | |
|---|---|---|---|
| 1 | shaping up | 6 | shove off |
| 2 | knock off | 7 | tumbles to |
| 3 | tuck in | 8 | bumps into |
| 4 | wrap up | 9 | swanning about |
| 5 | lashes out | 10 | wiped out |

## TEST 49

| | | | | | |
|---|---|---|---|---|---|
| 1 | c | built up | 6 | d | stuck up |
| 2 | d | throwaway | 7 | a | follow up |
| 3 | d | run down | 8 | d | see through |
| 4 | b | mixed up | 9 | d | takeover |
| 5 | b | worn out | 10 | a | stand offish |

## TEST 50

| | | | |
|---|---|---|---|
| 1 | bite off | 6 | wait for |
| 2 | throw out | 7 | comes out |
| 3 | turn over | 8 | runs away |
| 4 | cut off | 9 | look after/look after |
| 5 | put off | 10 | pick up |